Windows of the Heart

Silvia M. Mendez Robinson

VANTAGE PRESS
New York

Cover design by Polly McQuillen

FIRST EDITION

Published by Vantage Press, Inc.
419 Park Ave. South, New York, NY 10016

Manufactured in the United States of America
ISBN: 978-0-533-15898-0

Library of Congress Catalog Card No.: 2007906617

0 9 8 7 6 5 4 3 2 1

What already seems like a lifetime of felt emotions, I am not sure if I want to care and love as I have in the past the same way for the future. It has been too hurtful and too unloving of relationships I have had and experienced and . . . I have not truly had even with memories of fondness, tears, and smiles.

Windows of the Heart is dedicated to those who believe they are good and pure within their hearts of love for devoted relationships. It is what makes honesty prevail to whatever love one feels for a person or something.

It is also dedicated to those who have experiences that are similar and can relate to what hurt lies unfound.

Contents

To Live from the Heart

No man can touch my heart
Like the way you do.

Time after time I try to close
Down the emotions to try and
Stop the heartache.

While thinking of you, I remember
The times we shared as kids.

Playing in the park late at night
Singing to the sound of the sky,
Playing on the merry-go-round.

I love you, I love my heart and
The feelings I have for a special man.

Maybe I'll never know what it feels
Like to be in your arms, but I know
You'll always be in my heart.

Love lives on inside,
It's something I've tried to hide,
Until now.

A Kiss to Heal

A Kiss from one to tell the truth.
A Kiss from one to make me feel.
A Kiss from one to make me love notes.
A Kiss from one to help me heal.
A Kiss from one to let me know we've begun to run my trust fund.
A Kiss from one to know I was loved and am loved.
A Kiss from one to know I'm admired.
A Kiss from one to show me I'm desired.
A Kiss from one to remind me when I was young.
A Kiss from one to let me know I can sing.
A Kiss from one to let me know I'm your everything.
A Kiss from one to sing you still love me.
A Kiss from one to say I love you too.
A Kiss from one to spend a weekend together.
A Kiss from one to say I'm sorry for hurting you.
A Kiss from one to let me know we've just begun to share our lives together.
A Kiss from one to tell me I'll be safe, in any given place.
A Kiss from one to tell me he cares from past, present to future.
A Kiss from one to take away my fears and wipe away my tears.
A Kiss from one to tell me he's sorry for what he has done.
A Kiss from one to tell me he believes in us.
A Kiss from one to tell me he didn't deceive.
A Kiss from one to promise me I'll receive.
A Kiss from one to tell me we'll always be close.
A Kiss from one to travel from coast-to-coast.
A Kiss from one to love me as I am.
A Kiss from one to tell me he'll never leave, he's my lifelong dream.

A Kiss from one to promise to send flowers.
A Kiss from one to remind me to let myself heal.
A Kiss from one to promise not to steal.
A Kiss from one to ask me for my hand, a loving man.
A Kiss from one to help me to stay healthy and exercise.
A Kiss from one to promise to be my best friend.
A Kiss from one to tell me I'm still close and dear.
A Kiss from one to hold me all nights.
A Kiss from one to always be the light.
A Kiss from one to always say good night.
A Kiss from one to be my love and my man.
A Kiss from one to be my partner for life.
A Kiss from one to learn his way of fun.
A Kiss from one to be strong and let me walk along, by your side.
A Kiss from one to undress me for some fun, preferably my husband-to-be.
A Kiss from one to watch T.V. with late at night.
A Kiss from one to lay out at the beach.
A Kiss from one to massage my hands, legs and feet.
A Kiss from one to taste my passion as his wife.
A Kiss from one to cuddle when I want.
A Kiss from one to cook my favorite meal.
A Kiss from one to take me on a trip, sandals and sun.
A Kiss from one to surprise me with my eyes, more than between his passionate thighs.
A Kiss from one to hold my hand.
A Kiss from one to give me pleasure.
A Kiss from one to keep my measure.
A Kiss from one to satisfy in life.
A Kiss from one to take me to our place to gently hold each other face-to-face.
A Kiss from one to really know my favorite scent on me and on you, something rather pleasant.

A Kiss from one to really know what I meant when I'm upset.

A Kiss from one to let me sleep when I'm tired, because he knows he's admired.

A Kiss from one to change my tire, wash my car and fill it up with gas.

A Kiss from one to warm up by the fireplace.

A Kiss from one to laugh with throughout our life together.

A Kiss from one to giggle in the night.

A Kiss from one to know our passion, my passion.

A Kiss from one to know my style, my color, my fashion.

A Kiss from one to share our hobbies, our favorite, our dreams.

A Kiss from one to know what I don't like.

A Kiss from one to pleasantly surprise me.

A Kiss from one to love good things, quality and quantity.

A Kiss from one to know my silence.

A Kiss from one to dress to impress, to want to wear to arouse you at any time.

A Kiss from one to have breakfast with, my coffee mate.

A Kiss from one to know my favorite plate, my favorite drink.

A Kiss from one to buy me shoes I can actually use, no returns.

A Kiss from one to wiggle in my favorite gown or t-shirt.

A Kiss from one to light my candle, play our music and fluff our pillows.

A Kiss from one who'll warm my bubble bath, rub my bubbles, shampoo my hair, and powder me all over.

A Kiss from one to let me sit on his lap to watch T.V., sleep, munch, or nap.

A Kiss from one to let me change his clothes.

A Kiss from one to cook together wearing each other's apron.

A Kiss from one to love each other as man and wife till
    grandchildren tire us out.
A Kiss from one to be in pictures together as a couple.
A Kiss from one to take care of me for life.
A Kiss from one to be a dedicated spouse, always to arouse.
A Kiss from one to clean, paint and glue.
A Kiss from one to shop, shop and shop, for me, you and
    the children.
A Kiss from one to attend the sports games.

What Every Woman Should Know
(Loving a Wicked Man, Not to Be)

When a woman in love trusts everything the man she loves says.

When a woman in love makes the man in love feel like he is the only man in the place.

When a woman in love rushes home from work to be with the man she loves for all those (E) needs. (Remember E = erotic or E = exotic)

When a woman in love cooks the man she loves his favorite dinner and finishes with accidentally spilling the Bananas Foster on his lap for a passionate scrub and rub.

When a woman in love wants the man in love <u>happy and content</u> and agrees to certain events, situations, or ways to satisfy him like no other woman can!

When a woman in love sacrifices her desires, wants, needs, professional life for the man she loves to encourage or further his career because <u>he is everything</u> to her <u>in her world.</u>

When a woman in love holds the man in love's hands in a movie, at dinner, or simply walking in the park; of course, don't forget the mall.

When the woman in love buys her favorite cup of coffee "café vanilla" because it reminds her of the man she loves.

When the woman in love stays in the best possible shape for the man she loves so the man she loves is proud to be with her.

When the woman in love speaks about the man she loves is always positive, healthy and supportive.

When a woman in love waits to hear from the man in love after seeing him at a party (à la carte) and standing at a distance.

When the woman in love waits days, weeks, months, mostly years to receive flowers from the man she loves. Flowers mean much more than just a quick purchase. (To blossom)

When a woman in love smells the man in love's pillows and clothing to remind her of him waiting for the next time they see each other.

When the woman in love calls to leave a sweet message on the phone, voicemail to the man she loves letting him know that throughout the day she is thinking of him.

When a woman in love sends the man in love a Scooby snack to remember to stay healthy, letting him know that she is thinking about him.

When the woman in love loses her dream because the man in love doesn't think she deserves it, and hardly knew her then and realized he made a big mistake, because she did deserve it, the dream.

When the woman in love surprises the man she loves with a new home, new car or helps push him up the professional career ladder.

When the woman in love is hurt and is at the end of her desire, her loving spirit and the man in love just doesn't figure it out, (apologize) or if he has he isn't doing the right thing to bring it back and put her where she is supposed to be. (Elevator?)

When the woman in love is told by the man she loves to "go home," but yet since they haven't been together and is not sure what is home to him and not to be told by some other man.

When the woman in love searched for the man she loves left and is sure to be in some sort of trouble by him because she <u>was seen</u> by the loft and we weren't together, leaving him wonder what was she doing there? (Am I right?)

When the woman in love is still wondering about the man she loves' birthday.

When the woman in love considers the man she loves a necessity and not an accessory (otherwise, have many).

When the woman in love <u>loves</u> the man she loves so much and is a challenge that energizes the heart, cleanses the mind, lifts the body, calms the soul, quiets her fears, massages the skin, invigorates the body, sings her to sleep and brings her breakfast in bed.

When the woman in love thinks of the man she loves and writes everlasting, poems for our children's children's children to read.

When the woman in love is not with the man she loves during the holidays and misses the holiday spirit and family get together instead of it being just another day and alone.

When the woman in love tries to please the man she loves by

having his car washed, even though it may not meet his standards. (Drive through)

When the woman in love doesn't realize until after she resigns that the man she loves helped her get a job to start her in a positive career move. (Sorry)

When the woman in love trusts the man she loves to lawfully and not illegally change any property that is hers to anyone else's name or company name. Property being a noun, real estate, currency or item on the element chart.

When the woman in love takes <u>one</u> strand of garland down from a cubicle and sends the man she loves the person off to law school. This is a true punishment knowing it is a dream of mine, not once but twice.

When the woman in love tries to protect an African American female from someone writing "I have a dream" on a memo and intimidating her. After going through the proper human resources step with the employer and a third party staffing agency decides to leave even after apologizes and is then asked to leave because a man lied and said that he has slept with me. When some of the male employees did not want proper <u>structure</u> and policy, to set up a new office and the man in love never speaks to the true source to hear the truth, [but continues to punish].

When the woman in love has enough tragedy, enough shattered dreams, enough painful years for one person to write as much as I have so far when does it turn around, when does it stop, when do you stop blaming me and start blaming the people you really and truly need to face and some say hope the man she loves really tries to understand me and not ignore me.

When the woman in love is lied to by the man she loves who lied to the Duke of <u>Earl</u>?

When the woman in love is with friends and someone she cares about asks her to sit on his lap and does and the man in love <u>not yet known</u> by her how he feels tells her that if you sit on his lap, all your Christmases will be lonely and not happy. (You have been successful—proud? You have made Christmas like any other day.) Not deserved at all.

When a woman in love is asked a question by a man she loves and disrespects her tremendously by doing something again to shatter her dreams and gives it away to a woman who is not deserving (piano bar).

When a woman in love trusts the man she loves is truly not looking out for her, but for himself and it is all about and from the woman, otherwise the true and real existence of you, he is today would be different had it not been for the woman in love's intelligence—otherwise change your life to years ago as you have done to me.

When a woman in love is told she is a lesbian for having gone to a midnight gay bar and is told she would have to sleep with a woman. Absolutely no desire just out with a relative and not a love mate to have a good time and fun.

When a woman in love tells the man she loves she has been waiting a very long time for her blue sapphire because it is hers.

When the woman in love is always sacrificing and wants the man she loves to change the way to not only give, but to take what is lawfully and rightfully hers to be hers and his when married.

When the woman in love asks for the man she loves to give a massage and refuses, at a spa—(1/2 of <u>the party of 2</u> is the one giving the massage).

When the woman in love is surprised by the man she loves and builds special gifts for people because he is a loving man.

When a woman in love realizes the man she loves is truly a warm and loving man and that he really thinks she's special regardless of age.

When a woman in love is finally made aware by the man she loves by taking the time to show her how much he cares about her.

When the woman in love waits for the man she loves and he comes along from his past to set it straight and truly open his heart.

When the woman in love leaves the man she loves with all her heart to wait and have a baby with him regardless the age or time.

When the woman in love desires so much to remember what it's like, what it feels like to having her loving man next to her from night until morning, to actually roll over and feel a man not a pillow.

When a woman in love waits to take pictures, family pictures, portrait, and have more than three in the picture, a family complete.

When a woman in love wonders what kind of memories she will have with the man she loves, if at all.

When the woman in love respectfully tells the man she loves that he was disrespectful and he agrees and apologizes for his behavior (I love you more).

When a woman in love is in an elevator and no words are spoken but intense desire to . . . intense desire to feel you.

When a woman in love loves the man she loves and she wants to be in his world, world of pleasure.

When a woman in love loves the man she loves so intensely that she has to take a few minutes to run to the bathroom to freshen up.

When a woman in love loves the man she loves and wants to wear his favorite (teddy) lingerie.

When a woman in love is still waiting for her manicure from the man she loves.

When a woman in love arrives at a party alone and the man she loves startles her and then he leaves.

When a woman in love loves the man in love tries to explain their past as kids and then tells her to leave.

When the woman in love hears that the man she loves is in need or some sort of trouble and does anything she can to satisfy the need or help him out of trouble, even as kids.

When the woman in love finds out that a certain person is threatening the man she loves and asks the certain person through a third party to stop sexually hurting him because he is around me or talks to me. (It needs to stop!)

When the woman in love finds out that the man she loves is all about money and would rather stay in business than be with the woman he loves.

When the woman in love looks, searches for the man she loves throughout her day just to get a glimpse of him.

When the woman in love is told to leave by the man she loves and she realizes he is truly trying to protect her. (I love you.)

When a woman in love wants to call the man she loves for his birthday but was told only to call if it is an emergency.

When the woman in love is so afraid to call the man she loves but calls private or anonymously to say "Happy Birthday" but can only listen when she <u>hears</u> his voice and hangs up because it is not an emergency.

When a woman in love calls the man she loves to say "hi" and he is happy to hear your voice, but someone on the wireless line disconnects the call in the middle of the conversation changes to a land line and the wireless phone is too staticky within a ten (10) mile range.

When a woman in love is waiting to hear from the man she loves as months go by from an out-of-state graduation and gets a non-friendly text message. (That's upsetting.)

When the woman in love has to pump her own gas and she

was so appreciative and grateful when her husband of years ago would take the time to fill her car. (Those were one of the simple things I loved about being married; my safety was always on his mind to not ever be stranded anywhere because he cared.)

When a woman in love lets the man in love buy himself another toy, a fast motorcycle and get matching helmets, pictures and lets it sit in the garage collecting dust on the dust cover. (Wasn't the motorcycle for me?)

When the woman in love was <u>constantly</u> criticized for folding the towels the wrong way and would have to refold them the way he wanted them. (I was a great wife!! To put up with that.)

For a man in love to love the woman he loves so much that documents are changed to not give her the money that is lawfully hers as a beneficiary to keep her close to him because it is just his controlling nature.

For a woman in love to see and speak to the man she loves hasn't seen him for awhile, years, and realizes it was who he was a few hours later, a delayed reaction and cries alone because she realizes that he cares for her after all these years, but never married. (A true friendship to last a lifetime.)

When the woman in love smells the man she love's cologne and is thinking of him and not the man walking by.

When the woman in love walks in the home and smells the man she loves, she knows he's waiting for her.

When the man she loves finally realizes that his friends were wrong and the woman he loves is truly a very passionate loving woman.

When a woman in love standing on a pier and the man she loves and the man in love mysteriously appears to quietly and discreetly speak to her to tell her of future events of good, of bonding of the two hearts for so many years to not kiss, to not hold, to not touch, to know each other as kids and before the sand lot, one a baseball diamond, one a sandy beach to build Clearwater . . . family environment, to be sure of an answer to request and not to test, albeit a test of the quest, to honor and obey, to be sure one does not stay, so lonely, how about forgiveness? Yes to the quest, as test of the hearts did we depart a proposal on the pier, a heart so hurt to walk away, as he goes on to play. A man of honor, a man of creed, a man to have, a friend of his to be near, a tear or more that night a truly long drive to him, alone.

When a woman in love wants to touch the shoulder of the man she loves, but he walks too fast to touch or looks back and frightens you.

When a woman in love is sitting next to the man she loves and is waiting for him to put his hand on your lap or thigh to give you a gentle squeeze.

When a woman in love listens for her name and it is the man she loves calling her.

When the woman in love meets the man she loves in the morning and he walks with her starting out their day together.

When the woman in love wants to have a conversation with the man she loves and he holds all calls to say "hi."

When a woman in love has been without the man she loves for so long that she is not sure what to say, Silvia M. Robinson, what to do to start the conversation or to know if he is flirting or if he really wants her, when she is really not sure of the subtle gestures he is giving to know, to really know that he wants her.

When a woman in love is really hurting inside and is hoping the man she loves is understanding her enough to be gentle and warm and not distant or hurtful or thinking that he doesn't want him because she does, it's just what he said, "she hasn't been around the block yet."

Wicked, Not to Be
Part I

For a man to give a woman an STD on their first date, a one-night stand on purpose.

For a man in love to propose and then walk away.

For a man to not be with the woman he loves.

For a man to threaten a woman on a date to "have sex" or to be told they never will see the rest of their life on their first date.

For a man to promise to always be there to get you through and not hold on to their promise.

For a man to not honor his word.

For a man to threaten a struggling single mom to place their kids in foster care.

For a man to stalk a woman to ensure she is being ticketed for every possible reason.

For a man to make a toast of celebration and then to shatter and toss the champagne glasses to express his point.

For a man to call a woman a "bitch" when he really should be saying something nice.

For a man to know wrongs are being done and letting it continue and not taking action to correct the problem.

For a man to lie about sleeping with a woman (having sex) and hurting the true man that loves her and keeping them apart.

For a man to say he's confused about loving the right woman but knowing he's having sex with the wrong woman.

For a man to truly love a woman but stays away from her and sleeps with other women to not face his true emotions.

For a man in love to not tell the woman he loves how he feels, silence hurts.

For a man in love to stand right next to the woman he loves and letting her walk right by crying.

For a man in love to go along with the boys (guys) and not face the woman he loves even though he is hurting inside as she is the same.

For a man in love to not express in words, in a poem, a card, or a letter how he feels to the woman he loves.

For a man in love to continue hurting the woman he loves by not touching face-to-face, a kiss.

For a man in love to not share his friends and family with the woman he loves.

For a man in love to not share his goals, desires, mostly his accomplishments with the woman he loves to celebrate.

For a man in love to not celebrate with the woman he loves and yet being amongst many, alone himself, yet thinking of her.

For a man in love to know how he feels and not to express to the woman he loves, having her sitting home alone while he attends, social, holiday and evening events.

For the man in love to call the woman he loves not her name. Work must be pretty good & satisfying.

P.S. For a man in love not caring enough to be with the woman he loves for those special <u>tender</u> moments.

When a man in love blames the woman he loves for something she did not do, did not say, or was not with.

When a man in love leaves the woman he loves sitting in a bar or restaurant for over an hour and expects her not to be mad, or have any food or drinks while she is waiting for him.

When a man in love leaves the woman he loves sitting in a restaurant for an hour and has only excuses for his lateness and was out at a party.

When a man in love expects the woman he loves to be a graceful and smooth dancer and yet he won't dance with her. (Passion anyone?)

When a man in love needs to feel strong warm passion with the woman he loves and the graceful and smooth dancing happens naturally.

When the man in love asks the woman he loves to undress in front of a group of men to have sex and should truly be hot, passionate in love for only a party of two.

When the man in love tells the woman he loves to stop bothering him and she's just trying to undress him while he's watching a sports show.

When the man in love doesn't join the woman he loves for a scrub and rub in the tub. (Bubbles anyone?)

When the man in love has not yet with the woman he loves made love or painted her toenails, or . . . opened the gate, or shared a romantic picnic, (brie) or celebrated their first time they met or slowly undressed her placing perfume in the (E) areas . . . (E = erotic or E = exotic) your choice.

For a man in love to have an engagement ring for the woman he loves and not propose to her because he doesn't have the courage to make the lasting commitment. (Is this meant to be?)

For the man in love to talk negatively about the woman he loves because someone he knows is dating her or wants to date her and is trying to convince him not to date the woman he loves.

When the man in love is in a conference meeting with the woman he loves and doesn't speak his mind to avoid any criticism, and knowingly has others in the meeting put the woman he loves down to make her feel less in control or less intelligent. (Women do this too!)

For a man in love to let the woman he loves review her notes to bring her up-to-date since she has been out on maternity leave or ill or taking care of the children. (That's a loving man!)

For a man in love to stop by lunchtime to say hi and see how you are doing to the woman he loves (better than the voice mail message?).

When a man in love has an engagement ring for the women he loves and has not yet proposed because he is having thoughts or feelings of guilt of what an unloving man he is to continue to misuse her trust.

When a man in love tells the woman he loves she can send him an e-mail, but never responds back.

Wicked, Not to Be (Continued)
Part II

When a man in love loves his woman and tries to get her to understand or realize how much he loves her, but the woman he loves is so alone and getting used to not being loved or feeling loved that she makes mistakes not to hurt him but because she is so hurt and with doubt.

When a man in love wants to be with the woman he loves so much that when she makes a mistake he thinks she did it on purpose and does something hurtful to her again, when really all she wants to do is be with him in his arms.

When a man in love forgets what it's like to hug and hold the woman he loves affectionately.

When a man in love tries to get the woman he loves to come closer to him, but she is afraid of being alone, going the distance since she's been alone for far too long to have the courage (this is when the love support team is needed); [not a loud obnoxious, drinking, sex-it-up-late-night party]. {Tenderness is more meaningful than loudness.} The loudness is not a loving reminder when tenderness (tender moments) last a lifetime.

When a man in love tells the woman he loves he wants to marry her and doesn't give her a ring after more than a year, but yet follows her around as if she has done something wrong.

When a man in love wants to marry the woman he loves, but over a nine-year period, marries two other women. (Now

that's some serious love [confusion] going on.) Maybe coun-
seling might help?

When the man in love is wanting to make love to the woman
he loves, but won't take her out to a special place.

When a man in love recons the woman he loves, sees her, but
stays sitting, talking to another woman as if he doesn't see her,
looking at her straight into her eyes, the woman he loves says
his name, but remains silent and doesn't acknowledge her.
(What's your name & purpose? To ignore?)

When a man in love truly loves the woman he loves, has never
been with her, talks about her, looks out for her safety, and yet
hasn't shared a touch together as one.

When a man in love needs to know that the woman he loves
truly loves him for all things that have yet been unsaid, uncele-
brated. (There's truth in touching and hugging to heal.) By the
way, I do, love you. When the man in love won't take the
woman he loves out on the boat because she just doesn't have
the perfect hourglass figure, shape.

When the man in love encourages and supports the woman he
loves professionally via verbally, and when she gets the job of a
challenge, he somehow calls the one friend that changes her
opportunity to failure. (Is this truly deserved?)

When the man in love wants to punish the woman he loves for
something she did but was years ago and were not yet a cou-
ple, but secretly continues to hurt her. (He's looking good, be-
having badly.)

When a man in love finally tells the woman he loves the truth about what a "fat bastard" he was regarding a certain situation. (The halls of USF.)

When the man in love doesn't do what's right with the woman he loves because he feels too guilty for what he did and stays away from her rather than face-to-face to tell her the truth (that sucks) because so many years have gone by.

When the man in love doesn't send flowers for years to the woman he loves to make a point, but yet doesn't truly express what is bothering him so the woman in love is given a chance to change for the man in love because she loves him so much [Is this too much or what?], especially when she is a good girl.

When a man in love makes things harder for the woman he loves to show her who is in control.

When a man in love hurts the woman he loves by not showing nurturing love to the woman's children.

When the man in love has friends take the woman he loves for six drinks to see if she can hold her liquor, doesn't serve food or tell her someone special is waiting for her until after the six drinks. (Inebriated comes to mind.)

When the man in love really screws up with the woman he loves by having the one friend he trusts to screw up on him by not truly caring for her and wanting her for him.

When a man in love makes his pregnant wife the woman he loves drive the Bronco II and not the Mercedes.

When the man in love takes the woman he loves to dinner in another city to threaten her she'll lose her children if she doesn't relinquish becoming mayor so he can place a different person of his choice and says she will marry no other man (Oreo cows—medium chubby boy).

For a man in love to use the woman he loves written poem as a conversation item instead of just talking to her because a) he is truly interested in her or b) he likes or write himself or c) she's a good looking woman (humor). All the above would be good instead of turning your car lights on at night when I get out of the car, I'm not sure if it's you or someone else is in the car and I value my safety.

For a man in love to copy or take a poem from the woman he loves (?) to send it off to be copyrighted by him and not me. (A short hockey poem.)

A Good Woman

If you are a good woman;
You are your own.
If you have loved a man and
He is no longer yours or is in heaven,
There is a feeling you have inside like
No other man gives you like the way he did.

It is a feeling inside that with others
You are very sad when you see
Couples happy. When you are by yourself
You feel his presence with you.
You want to fulfill your loyalty
Because that is what a good
Woman does, it's not revenge;

It is the love of the one love that gives
You the euphorical happiness when you
Were with him. It is a feeling inside
That you fail if you do not carry on his passion,
So you don't let another man inside you.

You want that passion safe unless and until
There is someone, a man that makes you feel again,
But you feel guilty of feeling the euphorical passion again,
You know it's there because how when you are alone
You want to be with the man that makes you feel the
Passion you once experienced.

So being alone is no longer a need, being a couple
Is what you yearn for with the new man of
Passionate feelings, you don't feel guilty you
Feel it is a continuance of the loyalty and passion.

It's just taking that step to get closer and letting
Yourself feel. It is o.k. after all you are a woman
And he a man, a mutual attraction, a puristic conception.
A mutual affection, a pleasure of once, body to body,
To share to see man upon, a moist treasure, to one foreplay,
A couple to sense all of each other no one else to that
matter.

Reflections of Love and Pain

Loving a man as much as you love your children, yet not able to share the warm and tender moments with him.

Giving a man all your love, heart and soul and waiting to know he feels the same.

Knowing the man you've loved all your life doesn't show the same love back from himself, but only through others.

Being around is something, being loved is one thing, being with him is all things.

Not knowing the difference a hug can make in a person's life.

Wanting to hug a man you care about, but can't find him, because he doesn't want to be found.

Loving a man that prefers to act as another, instead of being his own man.

Wanting the only arms that can heal you, but not able to tell him because he'd rather be around instead of bound.

Knowing the only man that can heal you and mend your pain, have the man tell you to "GO."

Living life hoping the man that promised to come and get you as a young girl holds true to his word.

Love is honoring your words; a true man stands his ground and honors his word to his true love, the woman who waits for him.

Knowing that time is so precious, not wanting a minute to go by without the one you love to share each moment and being in love and making memories.

New memories always keep the heart growing with curiosity and love for each other.

Love is . . . the man of your dreams come true and you satisfying his dreams.

Commitment to his love and children for life on heaven and earth and earth and heaven.

Wanting to build each other's memories from dreams.

Wanting to know his love and worries as he knows yours.

Being one with each other for good and better.

Knowing you are loved by your man.

Time is now to win your man.

Just giving each other enough space to know two make one.

Soothing his pain with the warm touch of your skin.

Saying "I love you" by staring eye-to-eye with the one who knows you most of your life.

Keeping the most tender moments in your heart as if it happened yesterday.

Giving the man your love, your heart with a child, who has his eyes.

Loving his children because they are the ones that let your love live on in lifetimes.

The love of his children loving you as your children do.

Helping him forget his pain of hurting you.

Forgiving him for the things he thought were fair, that hurt you deeply, and healing his conscience with love.

Knowing he's there, but wanting more, waiting for him to wrap his arms around you to know your world is safe and warm.

Counting the days to be together for the rest of your life.

Changing your ways without him asking, just knowing him well enough to know it is for the better.

Giving him time, time to realize how deeply in love you are with him and making him feel secure that it is for life.

Feeling his love and strength when he's standing next to you.

Letting him know you love him each and every day by the little things you do.

Loving you more by making me feel like a woman in those soft and tender moments.

A Couple to Come Closer

A Couple to become closer
To openly share a divine
Sense of purity's love.

A Couple to become closer
To openly share a nervousness
Of love's ultimate tradition.

A Couple to become closer
To openly share a passionate
Curiosity to pleasures together as one.

A Couple to become closer
To openly share a love's
Strengthening spiritual bond.

A Couple to become closer
To openly share an embrace
To control love's uncontrollable
Internal release of relaxing
Into each other's vulnerability.

A Couple to become closer
To openly share the sensation
Of internal penetration to
Everlasting honesty of
Each other's continuous need
To satisfy the fondness of one's heart.

A Couple to become closer
To openly share mutual
Tenderness of sensual
Touch that brings
Warm moments of
Internal expression.

A Couple to become closer
To openly share a healing
Of love's reflection of
Desirous need to reassure
Each other are one.

A Couple to become closer
To openly share an
Intensely alluring admiration
Of perfecting pleasure to
One another.

A Couple to become closer
To openly share an appealing
Sensibility of limitless
Postures of natural intimacy.

A Couple to become closer
To openly share a private escape.

A Couple to become closer
To embellish one's adoring,
Loving inner sweetness
Of taste to season the
Skin's flavor.

A Couple to become closer,
To experience exotic
Delicate sensation of
Unique luxury of
Unpredictable orgasmic
Emotion.

More Than Living in the Moment

Sharing my love and
Feeling you is more than
Living in the moment.

Loving you all the ways
To make you happy is more than
Living in the moment.

Being your "Good Woman"
And better to satisfy
The needs you have is more than
Living in the moment.

To give you the highest
Pleasure and you give it
Back to me is more than
Living in the moment.

To receive your love each day
Of pleasure is more than
Living in the moment.

Caressing your body, your skin;
The sweet taste of love,
The supple scent of your love,
The passionate movement of
Your love . . . is more than
Living in the moment.

Calm and gentle, you
Place me for soothing
Excitement, so thoughtful
Of my every bodily move
Is more than
Living in the moment.

Tender and sensual a motion
To signal a sexual emotion
Overwhelming to hold
Is more than
Living in the moment.

Holding me close and
Feeling me bloom, a
Radiance, a glow to
Express the multiple warmth
Is more than
Living in the moment.

A Love for All Seasons

A love for all seasons,
All love for many reasons
With kindness compassion.

When a possibility is loved
By one and wanting of a
Special man's touch
The thought persistently
Reflects to a possible dream;

But he responds with his
Masculine tone of "hold that
Thought and never let go," in
Front of many.
Don't ever let it go.

For one who dares,
That's quite rare
In beauty and love's
Purity shared,
In wishing upon a star
In the clear sky blue.

In beautiful days and
Wonderful events too,
Does a man and woman's
Dreams come true.

Inspiring mutual happiness
Do memories begin to exist
Made by a couple, two.

In virtue's honor and
Loyalty's commitment,
In a handsome man's heart
And a beautiful woman's emotions
Clearly throughout the years
Does love grow closer and fonder.

In hopes to bring them closer,
To share his future plans
To find a loving day
Of celebration with two hearts
Of same love and caring
Intimacy does one find a
Light to come together
In love and strength,
In unity and fondness,

A Love for All Seasons

Sharing,
Tenderness,
Lover Everlasting.

A Love for All Seasons.

Inspiration Can Be . . .

Inspiration
    Can be in a Moment

Inspiration
    Can be in a Lifetime

Inspiration
    Can be a Man

Inspiration
    Can be a Woman

Inspiration
    Can be a Child

Inspiration
    Can be a Relationship
    Fulfilled in Love and in Honor

Inspiration
    Can change the world to a Loving Land

Inspiration
    Can be when all of us take the same Stand

Inspiration
    Can be quite grand when we make a movement
    To better this nation's world land.

A Lineage

It is a trust of relation.
     It is about preservation, utmost.
It is about beauty, and love
     It is about thee.
Always have a watchful eye.

You are a man of finesse
     A man quite grand
Do stand to be honored,
     To be known, you are
Now the highest of your throne.

'Tis yourself quality pleasure,
     Nonetheless, of
Transportation, foods, entertainment,
     Arts, life of family, life of families,
Of your noblest man, loyalist,
     Trustworthy friends, and
To your people be no other, but
     Your genuine and divine self,

To this they will love and
     Support you in all that you
Must accomplish.

This may already be known, however
     Strong and well known, learn from
The littlest, learn from the elder,
     Learn from close and learn from afar,
Kindness will always be yours and everlasting.

To seek a noble
To seek a knight,
To seek the lands,
    To seek more

Of the edge of the knowing,
To dabble in the unknown,
To be most knowledgeable,
You are and will be a new

Leader of those,
To be a statue of the
New quality man,
A giver of life, love
And fulfillment.

To this they honor, as your
Judgment will be your
History of events to come,
So forth as you go be
With dignity in unison
And celebrate with many,
Celebrate with few the
Accomplishments of new
Long live your happiness,
    In thoughts.

Such Is
(Inspired from my visit to the Library of Congress 12.7.05)

A Special face that passes by.

Such is <u>Beauty</u>
To inspire mankind's
Creativity.

Such is <u>Honor</u>
To represent all branches
Of the Armed Forces.

Such is <u>Innocence</u>
To remind many of truth
In Events of History.

Such is <u>Creativity</u>
To breed research and
Development to
Unlimited potential.

Such is <u>Kindness</u>
To share for all
Country's diplomacy.

Such is <u>Virtue</u>
To remain strong for all
(Those/Others) in need.

Such is <u>Assertiveness</u>
To change the habits to
Begin to form the new era.

Such is <u>Destiny</u>
Of man to renew life.

Such is <u>Success</u>
In the betterment of justice.

Such is <u>Family</u>
To grow in love and trust.

Such is <u>Life</u>
To live for fulfilling & building
Loving relationships.

Such is <u>Dreams</u>
To be given by
One of purest love.

Such is <u>Creed</u>
To follow by one's
Heart & loyalty.

Such is <u>Eternity</u>
A forever lasting nurturing
Warmth from the heart.